A Guide to
AMERICAN STATES

North Carolina

THE TAR HEEL STATE

MEDIA ENHANCED BOOKS
AV2 BY WEIGL
ADDED VALUE • AUDIO VISUAL

www.av2books.com

AV² provides enriched content that supplements and complements this book. Weigl's AV² books strive to create inspired learning and engage young minds in a total learning experience.

Your AV² Media Enhanced books come alive with...

 Audio
Listen to sections of the book read aloud.

 Key Words
Study vocabulary, and complete a matching word activity.

 Video
Watch informative video clips.

 Quizzes
Test your knowledge.

Embedded Weblinks
Gain additional information for research.

 Slide Show
View images and captions, and prepare a presentation.

Try This!
Complete activities and hands-on experiments.

... and much, much more!

Go to **www.av2books.com,** and enter this book's unique code.

BOOK CODE

K 9 9 1 7 5 3

AV² by Weigl brings you media enhanced books that support active learning.

Published by AV² by Weigl
350 5th Avenue, 59th Floor
New York, NY 10118
Website: www.av2books.com   www.weigl.com

Library of Congress Cataloging-in-Publication Data

Foran, Jill.
  North Carolina / Jill Foran.
    p. cm. -- (A guide to American states)
  Includes index.
  ISBN 978-1-61690-805-8 (hardcover : alk. paper) -- ISBN 978-1-61690-481-4 (online)
  1. North Carolina--Juvenile literature. I. Title.
  F254.3.F662 2011
  975.6--dc23

                    2011019031

Printed in the United States of America in North Mankato, Minnesota

052011
WEP180511

Project Coordinator Jordan McGill
Art Director Terry Paulhus

Photo Credits
Every reasonable effort has been made to trace ownership and to obtain permission to reprint copyright material. The publishers would be pleased to have any errors or omissions brought to their attention so that they may be corrected in subsequent printings.

Weigl acknowledges Getty Images as its primary image supplier for this title.

Contents

Charlotte is the largest city in North Carolina and one of the nation's leading financial centers.

Introduction

North Carolina is known as the Tar Heel State. Historians disagree about the origin of the nickname. Some believe that it dates back to colonial days, when North Carolina was a leading producer of tar. Others trace the name to the Civil War. During one battle, North Carolina's soldiers refused to retreat, as if their heels were glued to the ground with tar.

One of the original 13 states of the United States, North Carolina is rich with history. In 1587, it was the birthplace of the first child born of English parents in America. In 1776, it became the first colony to authorize a vote for independence from Britain.

Thousands of blooms adorn Asheville's Biltmore Estate during the spring Festival of Flowers.

One hundred years after the Wright Brothers' first flight at Kill Devil Hills, a working re-creation of the Wright Flyer showed how history was made in 1903.

Slavery played a major role in North Carolina's farm economy during the state's early years. African American slaves planted and harvested most crops. By 1860, one of every three North Carolinians was an African American slave. North Carolina fought on the Confederate side during the Civil War. After the Union won the war in 1865, slavery was **abolished** across the country. North Carolinians rebuilt the state quickly after the war. By the end of the 1800s, agriculture and other industries were once again prosperous.

In 1903, near Kitty Hawk, Wilbur and Orville Wright conducted the first successful airplane flight. Today, North Carolina continues to be a site of innovation. The state has become known for its excellent research facilities and its highly respected colleges and universities. These features, along with the state's beautiful scenery, attract millions of visitors and new residents each year.

Where Is North Carolina?

North Carolina is located along the Atlantic coast, in the southeastern United States. Its coastline is dotted with lighthouses, particularly along the treacherous Outer Banks, a chain of sandy islands along the coast. Situated on the easternmost point of North Carolina, Cape Hatteras has been the site of many shipwrecks.

There are many ways to get to North Carolina. Several major interstate highways run through the state, and secondary highways provide links to the state's towns and cities. Rail service is also available, with Amtrak passenger trains offering daily trips across the state. North Carolina has several international and regional airports. The busiest airports are in Charlotte and in Raleigh-Durham. The Charlotte Area Transit System, or CATS, opened its first light-rail line in 2007.

Travelers can also reach North Carolina by boat. The state has ports along the Intracoastal Waterway, which is a protected sailing route along the Atlantic coast.

A pioneer in aviation, North Carolina now has 74 publicly owned airports, including three major airline hubs.

The Outer Banks have been called the "Graveyard of the Atlantic" because of the thousands of ships that have run aground on their shallow sandbars.

I DIDN'T KNOW THAT!

The state flag was adopted in 1885. By law, the flag must be displayed at all public buildings, state institutions, and courthouses.

Some houses along the Outer Banks have been constructed out of the hulls of old shipwrecks. Others are decorated with items rescued from sunken ships.

North Carolina has the largest state-maintained highway system in the United States.

The Old North State is a nickname often applied to North Carolina. This nickname comes from the early 1700s, when the colony of Carolina was being divided. Since North Carolina was the older colony of the two, most people referred to it as Old North Carolina.

Two presidents were born in North Carolina. James K. Polk was born in Mecklenburg County, and Andrew Johnson was born in Raleigh.

Both North and South Carolina claim to be the birthplace of another president, Andrew Jackson.

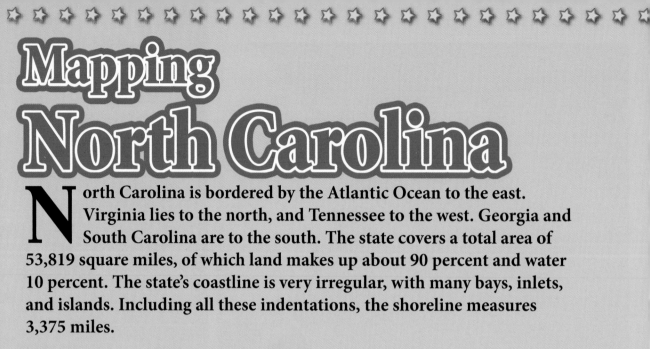

Mapping North Carolina

North Carolina is bordered by the Atlantic Ocean to the east. Virginia lies to the north, and Tennessee to the west. Georgia and South Carolina are to the south. The state covers a total area of 53,819 square miles, of which land makes up about 90 percent and water 10 percent. The state's coastline is very irregular, with many bays, inlets, and islands. Including all these indentations, the shoreline measures 3,375 miles.

Sites and Symbols

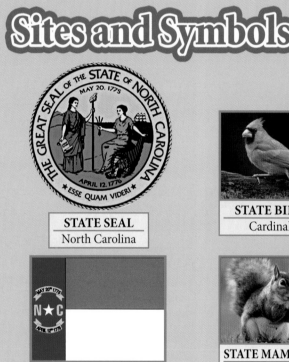

STATE SEAL
North Carolina

STATE FLAG
North Carolina

STATE BIRD
Cardinal

STATE MAMMAL
Gray Squirrel

STATE FLOWER
Dogwood

STATE TREE
Pine

Nickname The Tar Heel State

Motto *Esse Quam Videri* (To Be Rather Than to Seem)

Song "The Old North State," words by William Gaston, sung to a traditional melody arranged by Mrs. E. E. Randolph

Entered the Union November 21, 1789, as the 12th state

Capital Raleigh

Population (2010 Census) 9,535,483 Ranked 10th state

N

Map Scale

0   100 Miles

LEGEND

— Road
— River
⭐ State Capital
• City
▢ North Carolina
— State Border

STATE CAPITAL

North Carolina has had several state capitals. The first permanent capital, New Bern, was selected in 1766. Raleigh became the capital in 1792, and the state legislature began meeting there two years later. Today, Raleigh and nearby Durham and Chapel Hill form a metropolitan region with more than 1.2 million people. Access to Raleigh is provided by interstate highway, Amtrak rail passenger service, and Raleigh-Durham International Airport, which handles more than 9 million incoming and departing passengers annually. *Forbes* magazine recently listed Raleigh as the nation's best place for business and careers.

United States

Hawai'i   Alaska

North Carolina

The Land

North Carolina consists of three natural land regions. These regions are the Atlantic Coastal Plain, the Piedmont, and the Blue Ridge Mountains.

The Atlantic Coastal Plain extends along the Atlantic Ocean. The Outer Coastal Plain consists of low islands, hazardous offshore sandbars, grassy marshlands, large swamps, and shallow lakes. The Inner Coastal Plain features sand dunes, prairies, and some of the state's best farmland.

The Piedmont is located in the middle part of the state. It consists of gently rolling hills. Much of North Carolina's manufacturing and population are concentrated in this area. To the west of the Piedmont are the Blue Ridge Mountains. This region consists of steep mountain ranges and dense forests.

WHITEWATER FALLS

Located about 60 miles from Asheville, Whitewater Falls is the highest waterfall east of the Mississippi River.

GREAT DISMAL SWAMP

Since 1974, portions of the Great Dismal Swamp have been designated as a national wildlife refuge.

GREAT SMOKY MOUNTAINS

Great Smoky Mountains National Park is part of the Blue Ridge Mountains. It straddles the border between North Carolina and Tennessee.

OUTER BANKS

The Outer Banks are sandy barrier islands that extend about 200 miles along North Carolina's Atlantic coast.

The official state stone is the emerald. In 1970, the largest emerald ever discovered in the state was found in Hiddenite, near Statesville. The emerald weighed 1,438 carats and had a value of $100,000.

The Great Dismal Swamp, located in both Virginia and North Carolina, is the state's largest swamp. It covers an area of about 750 square miles.

North Carolina contains hundreds of waterfalls. The highest is Whitewater Falls, near Brevard, which is 411 feet tall.

Lake Mattamuskeet is the largest natural lake in North Carolina. This shallow lake measures 18 miles long by 7 miles wide. The lake is part of Lake Mattamuskeet National Wildlife Refuge.

Mt. Mitchell is the tallest peak in North Carolina, reaching 6,684 feet above sea level.

Powerful storms and surf batter the North Carolina coastline. Each year, shore communities must spend millions of dollars to restore seawalls and natural barriers.

Climate

Average January temperatures in North Carolina range from 40° to 45° Fahrenheit in most areas. In July the average temperature in the mountains is 68° F, while the average temperature for the rest of the state is 84° F. The highest temperature ever recorded in the state was 110° F in Fayetteville in 1983. The record low temperature was –34° F on Mt. Mitchell in 1985.

During summer and fall, North Carolina's coast is sometimes exposed to violent hurricanes. The worst hurrican disaster in North Carolina history was Hurricane Floyd in 1999, which caused billions of dollars in damage in the eastern part of the state.

Average Annual Temperatures Across North Carolina

Temperatures at Mt. Mitchell are much colder, on average, than those at Wilmington. What geographical factors account for the difference?

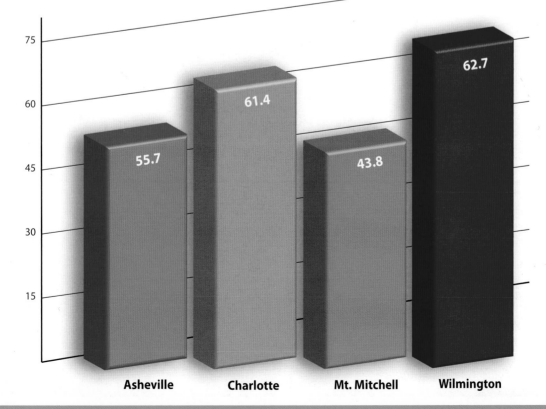

Degrees Fahrenheit

Asheville	Charlotte	Mt. Mitchell	Wilmington
55.7	61.4	43.8	62.7

North Carolina produces more than 5 percent of the nation's supply of lumber. The wood is used in housing and other types of construction.

Natural Resources

North Carolina's rich soil is one of the state's most important natural resources. The sandy soil found in the western and central parts of the Atlantic Coastal Plain is ideal for growing crops. The Piedmont also has productive soil. The most fertile soil in this region contains rich **alluvial** materials. North Carolina leads the nation in the value of its annual tobacco harvest.

Trees and water are the state's other important natural resources. Forests cover nearly three-fifths of the state, supplying raw materials for timber-related industries. North Carolina's lakes, rivers, and coastal waters teem with fish and other marine life. Some of the state's rivers serve as sources of **hydroelectricity**.

Pine trees are common throughout North Carolina. The pine became the official state tree in 1963.

Fishing contributes about $85 million yearly to North Carolina's economy. Among the state's most valuable fish and seafood catches are blue crabs, clams, shrimps, flounder, trout, and swordfish.

North Carolina streams and soil contain more than 300 types of rocks and minerals.

Tobacco is grown on more than 175,000 acres of North Carolina farmland.

Plants

North Carolina's dense forests contain many kinds of trees. Pines are plentiful on the Atlantic Coastal Plain. Hardwoods such as oak, ash, and hickory grow in the mountains. The Piedmont has a mix of evergreens and hardwoods. White cedars, black tupelos, and sweet gums grow in swamps and along rivers. The Black River area contains bald cypress trees. Some are 1,700 years old, making them the oldest known trees in the country east of the Rocky Mountains.

The Atlantic Coastal Plain is recognized for its distinctive plant life. About a dozen **carnivorous** plants grow in the state's swampy areas. One of the most interesting of these is the Venus flytrap. This plant traps insects by closing its leaves over them. It then digests them.

BALD CYPRESS

Bald cypress trees usually grow 50 to 100 feet tall and thrive in a wide variety of North Carolina soils.

FLOWERING DOGWOOD

Standing up to 30 feet tall, the flowering dogwood prefers partial shade and moist, well-drained soil.

VENUS FLYTRAP

After closing over an insect, the leaves of the Venus flytrap can take up to two weeks to digest their prey.

LILY

The Stargazer lily reaches heights of 3 feet or more and usually blooms in midsummer.

I DIDN'T KNOW THAT!

North Carolina's four national forests are Pisgah, Nantahala, Croatan, and Uwharrie. Together these forests cover more than 1.2 million acres.

North and South Carolina are the only places in the world where the Venus flytrap grows in the wild.

The Carolina lily was adopted as the state wildflower in 2003. It grows in forests, hills, and swamps.

The Biltmore Forest School, founded by Carl Alwen Schenck in the 1890s, was the country's first school of forestry.

The Fraser fir became the official state Christmas tree in 2005.

Animals

North Carolina is home to a wide range of animals. Mammals include bears, wildcats, deer, raccoons, and opossums. Thousands of black bears live in the western mountains and in parts of the Atlantic Coastal Plain. The coastal plain also serves as habitat for many reptile species, including the American alligator, the largest reptile in North America. Several thousand alligators live in the state's southeastern swamps and rivers.

Birds common in North Carolina include the cardinal, wren, mockingbird, chickadee, woodpecker, and warbler. Wild turkeys, quails, and doves are also found in abundance. During winter months, many bald eagles can be seen in Uwharrie National Forest. The eagles are attracted to the easy fishing that the forest's **reservoirs** offer.

Among the many fish species found in the state's lakes and rivers are trout, bass, perch, bluegill, and crappies. The coastal waters are home to sea trout, sharks, Atlantic croakers, blue crabs, and shrimps.

CARDINAL

The cardinal became the state bird in 1943. Primarily a seed eater, it also feeds on small fruits and insects.

WILD TURKEY

Wildlife experts succeeded in boosting the state's wild turkey population from 2,000 in 1970 to 150,000 by 2005.

BLACK BEAR

The maximum weight ever recorded for a bear in North Carolina is 880 pounds.

EASTERN BOX TURTLE

Adapted to a wide variety of habitats, eastern box turtles in North Carolina are most often found in damp, forested areas with plenty of underbrush.

The eastern box turtle became North Carolina's official state reptile in 1979.

The Plott hound was adopted as the official state dog in 1989. This breed, the only one known to have originated in North Carolina, once hunted wild boar.

Many kinds of snakes are found throughout North Carolina. Some of these reptiles, such as the rattlesnake and the water moccasin, are poisonous.

The largest alligator found in North Carolina measured 12 feet 7 inches from head to tail.

The beaches along the Atlantic coast are prime nesting grounds for loggerhead sea turtles.

Tourism

Every year, more than 9 million people visit Great Smoky Mountains National Park. The park covers more than 800 square miles and stretches over the border into Tennessee. Tourists travel to the park for outdoor activities such as mountain biking, hiking, and camping.

Visitors to North Carolina can take scenic drives along the Atlantic coast. Many vacationers travel to the coast to enjoy the unspoiled beaches, quiet resort towns, and majestic lighthouses of the Outer Banks. The tallest lighthouse in the United States is Cape Hatteras lighthouse. Built in 1870, it was moved in 1999 to protect it from the encroaching shoreline.

One of North Carolina's most popular historic sites is the Wright Brothers National Memorial at Kitty Hawk. This memorial stands near the location of their first successful motor-powered flight.

WHITEWATER ADVENTURES

The rugged rivers of western North Carolina can challenge even the most experienced kayakers and canoeists.

FORT RALEIGH

At the Fort Raleigh National Historic Site, **archaeologists** and historians continue to unravel the mystery of what happened to England's "Lost Colony" in the 1580s.

CAPE HATTERAS LIGHTHOUSE

More than 200 feet high, the Cape Hatteras Lighthouse overlooks Cape Hatteras National Seashore and the treacherous Diamond Shoals.

ASHEVILLE

Lush countryside, fine hotels, and top-quality cultural attractions make Asheville one of North Carolina's most popular resort regions.

Tourism contributes more than $15 billion to the state's economy every year. More than 360,000 jobs in North Carolina depend on the tourist industry.

The Great Smoky Mountains are named for the blue haze that lingers over their vegetation. The "smoke" is actually water vapor that is released by the plants into the air.

Visitors to Fort Raleigh National Historic Site can learn about the mysterious disappearance of the "Lost Colony" of more than 100 early English settlers in the 1580s.

Nearly 3 million vacationers each year make overnight visits to Asheville.

Industry

North Carolina is among the country's leading industrial states. Long-established manufacturing industries include textiles, wooden furniture, and cigarettes. Among North Carolina's newer industries are industrial machinery and computers, electronic equipment, and chemicals. Many companies have established high-technology research facilities in an area called Research Triangle Park, located near Raleigh, Durham, and Chapel Hill.

Industries in North Carolina
Value of Goods and Services in Millions of Dollars

Finance, insurance, and real estate now makes up the largest single segment of North Carolina's economy. What factors account for the rapid growth of this industry in recent decades?

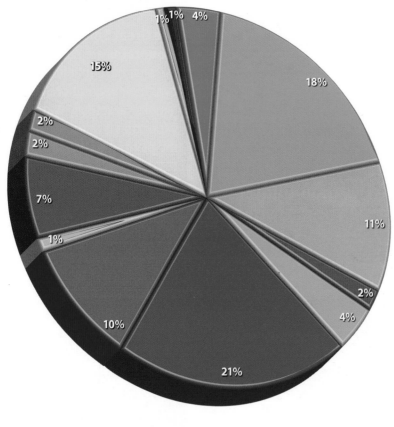

LEGEND

Category	Value
Agriculture, Forestry, and Fishing	$3,889
* Mining	$248
Utilities	$5,763
Construction	$15,617
Manufacturing	$72,371
Wholesale and Retail Trade	$42,890
Transportation	$8,683
Media and Entertainment	$15,419
Finance, Insurance, and Real Estate	$81,821
Professional and Technical Services	$40,800
Education	$3,872
Health Care	$27,251
Hotels and Restaurants	$9,820
Other Services	$9,189
Government	$60,409
TOTAL	**$398,042**

*Less than 1%. Percentages may not add to 100 because of rounding.

Agriculture was formerly the leading industry in North Carolina. Today, agriculture, forestry, and fishing employ a relatively small share of the work force. The main crops include tobacco, sweet potatoes, cotton, soybeans, corn, and peanuts. Livestock farms raise pigs, poultry, and cattle.

The first cotton mill in the state was built in 1813 near the town of Lincolnton.

North Carolina has hundreds of textile factories.

Sweet potatoes are a very important crop in North Carolina. The state leads the nation in sweet potato production, harvesting nearly two-fifths of the U.S. total.

Research Triangle Park is a 7,000-acre research facility that contains the offices and laboratories of more than 170 companies.

The textile industry is still one of the largest employers in North Carolina, although many jobs have been lost to foreign competition.

Goods and Services

North Carolina leads the country in the production of household furniture. High Point is nicknamed the Furniture Capital of the World. The High Point Market is the world's largest furniture trade fair.

Many of North Carolina's goods are exported to other states and countries. Chemicals are among North Carolina's most profitable exports. Factories throughout the state produce chemical products such as **pharmaceuticals**, plastics, **synthetic** fibers, and detergents.

A Diebold factory in Greensboro supplies banks throughout the United States with automated teller machines, or ATMs.

Training exercises at Camp Lejeune teach U.S. Marines how to deal with bomb attacks and other war hazards.

The 161-mile Wilmington-to-Raleigh Railroad was completed in 1840. At the time, this railroad was considered the longest in the world.

Durham, the home of Duke University, is a leading center for medical research.

The North Carolina *Gazette* was North Carolina's first newspaper. Printed in New Bern, the weekly paper was first published in 1751. It continued operations until 1761.

About three-fifths of the electric power generated in North Carolina comes from coal-burning power plants.

The world's first Krispy Kreme doughnut shop opened in Winston-Salem in 1937.

Banks, law firms, insurance companies, hotels, restaurants, and shopping malls provide service jobs for many North Carolinians. Government employees work at public hospitals, public schools, and military bases. Some of the country's largest military bases are located in North Carolina, including Fort Bragg, Camp Lejeune Marine Corps Base, and Seymour Johnson Air Force Base.

The University of North Carolina opened its doors at Chapel Hill in 1795, making it the first state-supported university in the country. Among the many other state-supported schools are North Carolina State University, in Raleigh, and the University of North Carolina School of the Arts, in Winston-Salem. Duke University, located in Durham, is the largest private university in the state and one of the nation's leading universities. North Carolina also has many technical institutes and community colleges.

American Indians

Prehistoric Indians lived in what is now North Carolina more than 15,000 years ago. Some early Indian groups established complex societies and constructed large earthen mounds. These ceremonial mounds were built by piling many layers of dirt on top of large pits. The mounds served as places of worship and burial sites.

Between 35,000 and 50,000 Indians were living in the North Carolina area when Europeans arrived in the 1500s. The Cherokee were the most numerous group when European settlements began. The Cherokee inhabited the mountains along the state's western border. Other major American Indian groups included the Catawba, the Tuscarora, and the Croatans.

Indians in North Carolina lived primarily in settled communities. The region offered abundant resources for food, clothing, and shelter. The Indians grew many crops, including beans, peas, melons, pumpkins, sunflowers, and potatoes. They lived in small buildings that they built of wood and covered with bark.

Cherokee weavers made baskets from river cane and other grasses. They also used honeysuckle, which was introduced to the South from Japan in the 1800s.

In addition to the foods they grew, the Cherokee gathered nuts, seeds, berries, and mushrooms from the surrounding countryside.

Today, the Lumbee are the largest Indian group in North Carolina. About 55,000 Lumbee live mainly in the south-central part of the state.

Town Creek, now a state historic site, has an Indian mound that was built around AD 1450.

Wanchese and Manteo, two American Indians from the North Carolina region, returned to England with Sir Walter Raleigh's expedition. In 1585, Raleigh sent Wanchese and Manteo back to North Carolina with 108 settlers so that they could act as interpreters.

The Tuscarora Indian War began in 1711. The Tuscarora were angry that European settlers had taken much of their land and accused the settlers of unfair trading practices. They attacked several settlements and killed many settlers. The settlers fought back and defeated the Tuscarora in 1713.

During the 1830s, most of the Cherokee were forced to move to Indian Territory, now Oklahoma. The journey is known as the Trail of Tears.

Explorers

The first European known to have explored North Carolina's coast was an Italian named Giovanni da Verrazzano. In 1524, Verrazzano wrote a report that described all of his findings. This report was sent to King Francis I of France, but the king made no attempt to colonize the region.

Spaniards were the next Europeans to explore the area. In 1540, a military expedition led by Hernando de Soto searched for gold in the mountains of southwestern North Carolina. Juan Pardo explored the same area in 1566 and 1567. Still, the Spanish made no attempt to settle the area.

England was the first European country to show interest in colonizing the North Carolina region. In 1584, Sir Walter Raleigh sent an expedition to choose a suitable site for a colony. When the explorers returned to England, they told Raleigh all about the Roanoke Island area, describing it with great enthusiasm.

A favorite of England's Queen Elizabeth, Sir Walter Raleigh gained his knighthood after sponsoring an expedition to North Carolina.

Timeline of Settlement

Early Exploration

1524 Giovanni da Verrazzano is the first European to explore the North Carolina coast.

1540 Hernando de Soto, a Spanish explorer, searches unsuccessfully for gold in the mountainous southwestern region.

First Settlements

1584 Queen Elizabeth I of England issues a charter to Sir Walter Raleigh to begin establishing colonies in North Carolina. During the next several years, boatloads of English colonists reach Roanoke Island.

1590 After a prolonged absence the colonial governor, John White, returns to Roanoke Island to find that the entire colony has disappeared.

1655 Fur trader Nathaniel Batts settles at the western end of Albemarle Sound.

Colonial Development and American Revolution

1705 French Protestants from Virginia establish Bath, the first town in North Carolina.

1766 New Bern becomes North Carolina's first permanent capital.

1776 On April 12, North Carolina becomes the first state to vote in favor of independence from Britain.

Statehood and Civil War

1789 On November 21, North Carolina is the 12th state to join the Union.

1792 Raleigh is designated as North Carolina's new capital.

1861 North Carolina secedes from the Union and then sides with the Confederacy during the Civil War.

1868 On July 4, North Carolina is readmitted to the Union as a state, three years after the Civil War ends with the Confederacy's defeat.

Early Settlers

In 1585, Sir Walter Raleigh sent 108 settlers to establish a colony on Roanoke Island. By 1586, food shortages and conflicts with Indians had forced the colonists to return to England. Eighteen men stayed behind to protect England's claim to the land. In 1587, Raleigh sent a second group of settlers to Roanoke Island. Upon their arrival in July, all that was left of the 18 men were a few skeletons.

Map of Settlements and Resources in Early North Carolina

4 *Pine trees growing in the Atlantic Coastal Plain provided raw materials for constructing settlements and for making boats watertight.*

1 *The first English colony in the New World was established on Roanoke Island in the 1580s. By the end of the decade, all the settlers had vanished.*

5 *The fur trade attracted some Virginians to move southward into North Carolina.*

2 *Bath, the first town in North Carolina, was established in 1705.*

6 *North Carolina's soil was well suited to tobacco growing, which was important in colonial times and increased rapidly after the Civil War.*

3 *Raleigh, a planned community, became the state capital in 1792.*

N

Scale

0   100 Miles

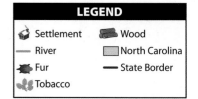

LEGEND		
Settlement		Wood
— River		North Carolina
Fur		— State Border
Tobacco		

By the end of August the second group was running out of supplies. The governor of the colony, John White, sailed back to England for more provisions. He was forced to stay in England for three years because the country's war with Spain kept him from sailing out of English ports. When White finally returned to Roanoke Island in 1590, there was no sign of life. The entire colony had mysteriously disappeared. Today, Roanoke Island is known as the Lost Colony. The disappearance of the settlers remains a mystery.

Eventually, farmers and traders from Virginia began moving southward into North Carolina. During the 1700s, the number of colonists increased rapidly, and settlement spread westward.

Born and baptized on Roanoke Island in 1587, Virginia Dare disappeared with all the other settlers of the Lost Colony.

I DIDN'T KNOW THAT!

On August 18, 1587, John White's granddaughter was born on Roanoke Island. Called Virginia Dare, she was the first baby born to English parents in America. A bridge named in her honor opened in 2002, linking Roanoke Island with the mainland.

When John White returned to Roanoke Island in 1590, he found the word "croatan" carved into a post and "cro" carved into a tree.

North Carolina and South Carolina were governed jointly from 1663 to 1712, when the two were separated.

The first legislative assembly in North Carolina met in 1665.

Blackbeard the pirate attacked ships off the North Carolina coast until he was killed in 1718.

A gold rush began in 1799 when gold was discovered in Cabarrus County.

Notable People

North Carolinians have excelled in many different fields, including politics, journalism, technology, literature, and music. Religious leaders and sports superstars have also made their homes in the Tar Heel State.

ANDREW JOHNSON (1808–1875)

Andrew Johnson grew up in North Carolina but pursued a political career in Tennessee. Although he was a southerner, he refused to support the Confederacy during the Civil War. Chosen by President Abraham Lincoln to run for vice president in 1864, Johnson became president a year later when Lincoln was shot to death. Johnson's political opponents **impeached** him but were unable to remove him from office.

EDWARD R. MURROW (1908–1965)

A native of Greensboro, Edward R. Murrow was one of the most admired American radio and television journalists of the mid-20th century. He risked his life reporting from London while Germany was bombing Britain during World War II. Later, his reports for CBS News spotlighted ways in which American society was not living up to its ideals.

BILLY GRAHAM
(1918–)

Raised on a farm near Charlotte, Billy Graham became one of the world's best-known Protestant ministers and preachers. His Christian message has reached hundreds of millions of people through books, radio, television, newspapers, magazines, and revival meetings. Graham has met and prayed with 12 U.S. presidents.

JOHN COLTRANE
(1926–1967)

John Coltrane learned to play horn and clarinet while he was growing up in High Point, and he began playing saxophone while in high school. He played with Dizzy Gillespie and Miles Davis before forming his own band. He blazed new trails for jazz in emotionally intense and harmonically daring works such as "A Love Supreme."

MAYA ANGELOU
(1928–)

Born in Missouri, Maya Angelou received a lifetime appointment in 1981 as professor of American studies at Wake Forest University. Before that, she became known as a civil rights leader, poet, and nonfiction writer. Angelou's most honored work, *I Know Why the Caged Bird Sings*, describes her childhood and teenage years.

I DIDN'T KNOW THAT!

The Wright Brothers, Wilbur (1867–1912) and Orville (1871–1948), grew up in the Midwest, but they made history in North Carolina. First they experimented with **prototype** kites and gliders made out of bicycle parts. Based on these experiments, they built the world's first functional airplane. On December 17, 1903, they made the first successful airplane flight.

Michael Jordan (1963–) was born in New York but grew up in Wilmington, North Carolina. He starred in college basketball with the University of North Carolina at Chapel Hill. Later, he led the Chicago Bulls to six professional championships. Today, he owns the Charlotte Bobcats of the National Basketball Association.

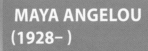

Population

North Carolina is one of the nation's fastest-growing states. The population of North Carolina increased 21.4 percent between 1990 and 2000 and 18.5 percent between 2000 and 2010. Today, more than 9.5 million people live in the state.

The state's population is highly diverse. African Americans make up about 22 percent of the total. Many Hispanics have come into the state, and Hispanic Americans now account for nearly 8 percent of the population. More than 100,000 American Indians live in North Carolina, which has one of the highest Indian populations of any state.

North Carolina Population 1950–2010

Almost 3 million more people lived in North Carolina in 2010 than in 1990. What actions do state and local governments need to take in order to keep pace with such rapid population growth?

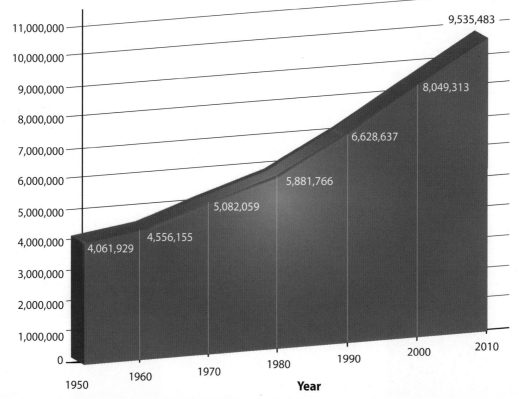

Number of People

- 4,061,929 (1950)
- 4,556,155 (1960)
- 5,082,059 (1970)
- 5,881,766 (1980)
- 6,628,637 (1990)
- 8,049,313 (2000)
- 9,535,483 (2010)

Year

North Carolina has one of the largest **rural** populations in the United States, although the number of people living in urban areas has increased in recent decades. About 40 percent of all North Carolinians live in rural areas.

The Piedmont region is home to the highest concentration of people. This region contains North Carolina's largest cities. Charlotte has the largest population, followed by Raleigh, Greensboro, Winston-Salem, Durham, and Fayetteville.

Raleigh, the state capital, has a population of about 400,000.

About 5 percent of North Carolina's population was born in a foreign country.

Charlotte, with more than 700,000 people, is the largest city in North Carolina. It was named after Queen Charlotte, the wife of King George III of England.

North Carolina is divided into 100 counties.

Population experts predict that North Carolina will have more than 12.2 million people by 2030.

Wake Forest, a suburb of Raleigh, is one of the fastest-growing areas of North Carolina. With more than 27,000 residents, the town has more than doubled in population since 2000.

The state capitol building in Raleigh was completed in 1840. Construction cost about $533,000, which was more than three times the state government's annual income at that time.

Politics and Government

North Carolina's government is divided into three branches. The legislative branch makes the state's laws. It consists of a 50-member Senate and a 120-member House of Representatives. Together these groups of lawmakers are known as the General Assembly. All members of the General Assembly are elected to two-year terms.

The executive branch makes sure that the state's laws are carried out. The governor heads this branch and is elected to a four-year term. Other elected members of the executive branch include the lieutenant governor, secretary of state, state treasurer, and state auditor.

The judiciary is the third branch of North Carolina's government. It ensures that North Carolina's laws are obeyed. The highest court in the state is the Supreme Court. It has six associate justices and a chief justice.

North Carolina's state song is called "The Old North State."

Here is an excerpt from the song:

*Then let all those who love us,
    love the land that we live in,
As happy a region as on this
    side of heaven,
Where plenty and peace, love
    and joy smile before us,
Raise aloud, raise together
    the heart thrilling chorus.
Hurrah! Hurrah! the Old North
    State forever,
Hurrah! Hurrah! the good
    Old North State.*

Until 1996, North Carolina was the only state that did not allow the governor to veto a bill passed by the General Assembly.

Judges on the North Carolina Supreme Court are elected by the voters to eight-year terms.

Born in Salisbury, Elizabeth Hanford Dole headed the U.S. departments of Transportation and Labor. She also served as a U.S. senator from North Carolina and president of the American Red Cross.

Cultural Groups

The early European settlers in North Carolina represented a variety of nationalities, including English, Scottish, Irish, and German. Their descendants make up the majority of the state's people. German Protestants known as Moravians first immigrated to Pennsylvania before settling in North Carolina. One of the first communities established by the Moravians was Salem, which was founded in 1766 and is now known as Old Salem. A replica of the original settlement is a popular tourist site where visitors can learn about Moravian life in 18th-century North Carolina.

One of the largest American Indian reservations in the United States is located on the western edge of North Carolina. Cherokee Indians share their early heritage at Oconaluftee Indian Village, which is located on the reservation. Here, visitors can watch Cherokee craftspeople demonstrate traditional arts and crafts.

Raleigh, which is 30 percent African American, holds a parade each January to honor the memory of Martin Luther King, Jr.

Civil rights groups in North Carolina succeeded in ending segregation at lunch counters in Greensboro and elsewhere.

African Americans have made major contributions to all aspects of life in North Carolina. African Americans honor their heritage in museums such as the African American Cultural Complex in Raleigh. In the 1950s and 1960s, African Americans in North Carolina played a pivotal role in the American **civil rights movement**. One of the most notable events happened on February 1, 1960, when four African American college students staged a sit-in at the **segregated** lunch counter in a Woolworth's store in Greensboro. The students sat at the lunch counter and were refused service, but they did not leave their seats until the restaurant closed. Then they returned the next day and did the same thing. Throughout the week more people joined the protest. The store closed its doors for a time, but in July it began serving African Americans. The sit-in served as a model for other protests against segregation throughout the South.

Arts and Entertainment

North Carolina has been home to many talented artists and performers. One of the state's best-known actors is Andy Griffith. He was raised in Mount Airy and starred in many popular television series, including *The Andy Griffith Show*. Born in Grabtown in 1922, Ava Gardner starred in numerous Hollywood films, including *Show Boat* and *The Sun Also Rises*.

Many gifted visual artists come from North Carolina. Bob Timberlake, a native of Lexington, is known for his beautifully detailed paintings. His work can be seen in museums across the country. The North Carolina Museum of Art, located in Raleigh, features an artwork collection ranging from ancient Egyptian pieces to contemporary works.

North Carolina has a strong literary tradition. Novelist and playwright Thomas Wolfe was born in Asheville in 1900. Short-story writer William Sydney Porter, who wrote under the **pen name** O. Henry, was born in Greensboro in 1862. His stories, widely read in the 20th century, were known for their surprise endings.

A member of the Rock and Roll Hall of Fame, James Taylor has recorded popular favorites such as "Fire and Rain," "You've Got a Friend," and "Carolina on My Mind."

Many celebrated musicians have hailed from North Carolina. John Coltrane ranks as one of the greatest saxophone players, composers, and bandleaders in jazz history. Other musicians who have been born or raised in the state include Nina Simone, Roberta Flack, James Taylor, Ryan Adams, and Ronnie Milsap.

Singer Nina Simone drew on jazz, blues, folk, and gospel traditions.

Set in North Carolina, The Andy Griffith Show *starred Griffith as Sheriff Andy Taylor. The long-running hit series also featured the young Ron Howard as Opie, Don Knotts as Deputy Barney Fife, and Jim Nabors as Gomer Pyle.*

Sports

North Carolina's mountains and seacoast offer excellent recreational opportunities. The state's four national forests and dozens of state parks feature hiking and mountain biking trails and other outdoor challenges. Rock climbers scale the vertical cliffs at Hanging Rock State Park, while hang gliders soar over massive sand dunes at Jockey's Ridge State Park.

The state's coastal areas are havens for those who enjoy sea kayaking, windsurfing, scuba diving, and other water sports. Long stretches of unspoiled beaches along the Outer Banks are also popular spots for sunbathing and swimming. Many rivers in the state offer excellent opportunities for whitewater rafting, and the scenic lakes are ideal for canoeing.

Many famous athletes have been associated with North Carolina. World-renowned boxer Sugar Ray Leonard was born in Rocky Mount and raised in Wilmington. During his impressive boxing career, he won several world titles and an Olympic gold medal. Dale Earnhardt, Sr., born in Kannapolis, was one of the most dominant **NASCAR** drivers of the 1980s and 1990s. His son, Dale Earnhardt, Jr., has also won a wide following among NASCAR fans.

Dale Earnhardt, Jr., was voted NASCAR's most popular driver eight years in a row, from 2003 to 2010.

College basketball is one of the most popular team sports in the state. North Carolina is home to four college basketball teams in the Atlantic Coast Conference. The four are the University of North Carolina Tar Heels, the Duke Blue Devils, the North Carolina State University Wolfpack, and the Wake Forest University Demon Deacons. Among the state's professional teams are the Charlotte Bobcats of the National Basketball Association, the Charlotte Sting of the Women's National Basketball Association, the Carolina Panthers of the National Football League, and the Carolina Hurricanes of the National Hockey League.

Named "Fighter of the Decade" in the 1980s, Sugar Ray Leonard entered the International Boxing Hall of Fame in 1997.

National Averages Comparison

T he United States is a federal republic, consisting of fifty states and the District of Columbia. Alaska and Hawai'i are the only non-contiguous, or non-touching, states in the nation. Today, the United States of America is the third-largest country in the world in population. The United States Census Bureau takes a census, or count of all the people, every ten years. It also regularly collects other kinds of data about the population and the economy. How does North Carolina compare to the national average?

Comparison Chart

United States 2010 Census Data *	USA	North Carolina
Admission to Union	NA	November 21, 1789
Land Area (in square miles)	3,537,438.44	48,710.88
Population Total	308,745,538	9,535,483
Population Density (people per square mile)	87.28	195.76
Population Percentage Change (April 1, 2000, to April 1, 2010)	9.7%	18.5%
White Persons (percent)	72.4%	68.5%
Black Persons (percent)	12.6%	21.5%
American Indian and Alaska Native Persons (percent)	0.9%	1.3%
Asian Persons (percent)	4.8%	2.2%
Native Hawaiian and Other Pacific Islander Persons (percent)	0.2%	0.1%
Some Other Race (percent)	6.2%	4.3%
Persons Reporting Two or More Races (percent)	2.9%	2.2%
Persons of Hispanic or Latino Origin (percent)	16.3%	8.4%
Not of Hispanic or Latino Origin (percent)	83.7%	91.6%
Median Household Income	$52,029	$46,574
Percentage of People Age 25 or Over Who Have Graduated from High School	80.4%	78.1%

*All figures are based on the 2010 United States Census, with the exception of the last two items. Percentages may not add to 100 because of rounding.

How to Improve My Community

Strong communities make strong states. Think about what features are important in your community. What do you value? Education? Health? Forests? Safety? Beautiful spaces? Government works to help citizens create ideal living conditions that are fair to all by providing services in communities. Consider what changes you could make in your community. How would they improve your state as a whole? Using this concept web as a guide, write a report that outlines the features you think are most important in your community and what improvements could be made. A strong state needs strong communities.

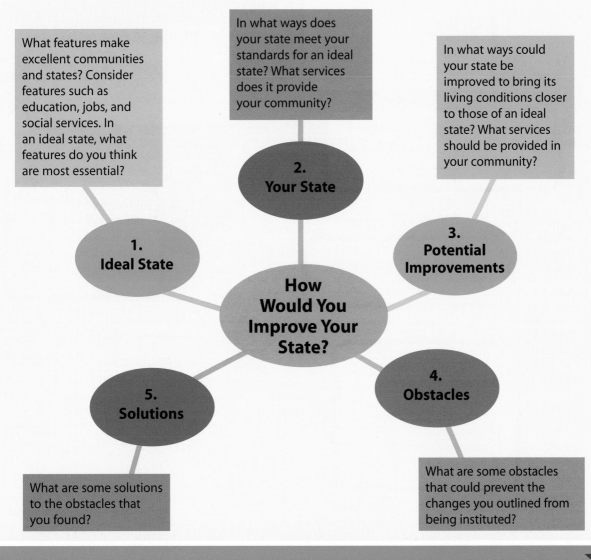

What features make excellent communities and states? Consider features such as education, jobs, and social services. In an ideal state, what features do you think are most essential?

In what ways does your state meet your standards for an ideal state? What services does it provide your community?

In what ways could your state be improved to bring its living conditions closer to those of an ideal state? What services should be provided in your community?

2. Your State

1. Ideal State

3. Potential Improvements

How Would You Improve Your State?

5. Solutions

4. Obstacles

What are some solutions to the obstacles that you found?

What are some obstacles that could prevent the changes you outlined from being instituted?

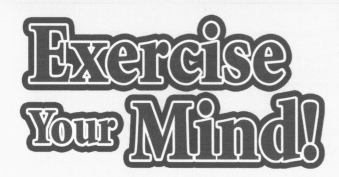

Think about these questions and then use your research skills to find the answers and learn more fascinating facts about North Carolina. A teacher, librarian, or parent may be able to help you locate the best sources to use in your research.

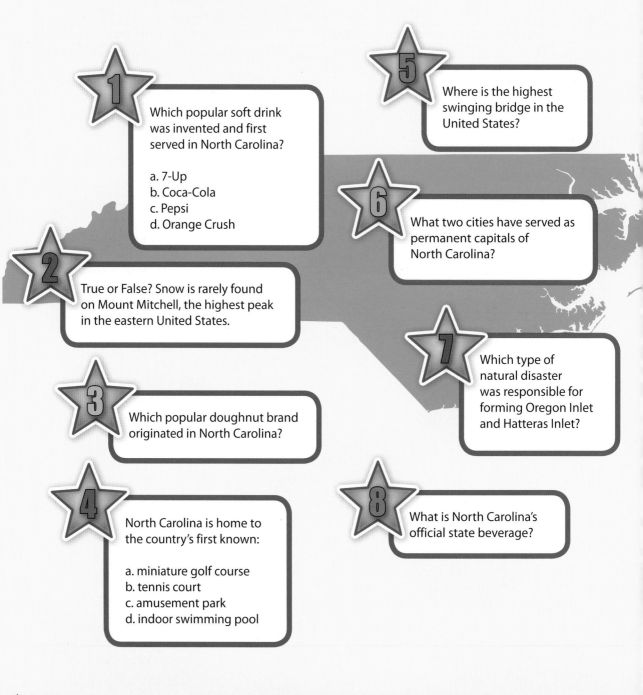

1 Which popular soft drink was invented and first served in North Carolina?

a. 7-Up
b. Coca-Cola
c. Pepsi
d. Orange Crush

2 True or False? Snow is rarely found on Mount Mitchell, the highest peak in the eastern United States.

3 Which popular doughnut brand originated in North Carolina?

4 North Carolina is home to the country's first known:

a. miniature golf course
b. tennis court
c. amusement park
d. indoor swimming pool

5 Where is the highest swinging bridge in the United States?

6 What two cities have served as permanent capitals of North Carolina?

7 Which type of natural disaster was responsible for forming Oregon Inlet and Hatteras Inlet?

8 What is North Carolina's official state beverage?

Words to Know

abolished: ended

alluvial: deposits of clay or sand left behind by flowing water

archaeologists: scientists who study early peoples through artifacts and remains

carnivorous: flesh-eating

civil rights movement: the struggle to achieve racial equality for African Americans

hydroelectricity: the production of electricity through waterpower

impeached: formally charged with wrongdoing

NASCAR: National Association for Stock Car Auto Racing

pen name: an assumed name used by a writer

pharmaceuticals: drugs and medicines

prototype: the first of its kind, used as a model

reservoirs: places where water is collected and stored

rural: relating to the countryside

segregated: racially separated and restricted

synthetic: artificially made

Index

Log on to www.av2books.com

AV² by Weigl brings you media enhanced books that support active learning. Go to www.av2books.com, and enter the special code found on page 2 of this book. You will gain access to enriched and enhanced content that supplements and complements this book. Content includes video, audio, web links, quizzes, a slide show, and activities.

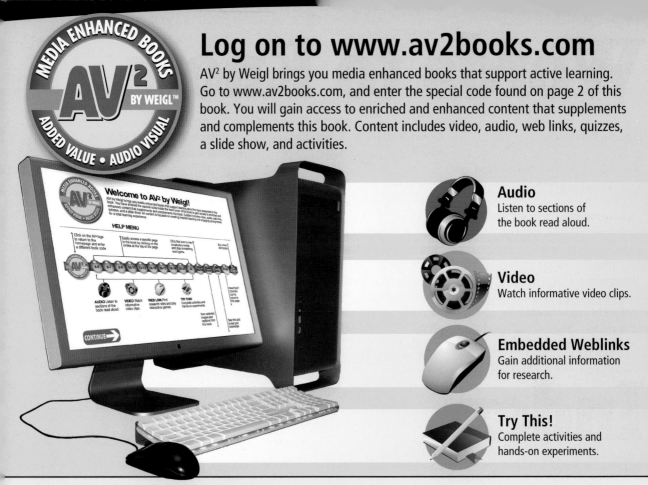

Audio
Listen to sections of the book read aloud.

Video
Watch informative video clips.

Embedded Weblinks
Gain additional information for research.

Try This!
Complete activities and hands-on experiments.

WHAT'S ONLINE?

Try This!	Embedded Weblinks	Video	EXTRA FEATURES
Test your knowledge of the state in a mapping activity.	Discover more attractions in North Carolina.	Watch a video introduction to North Carolina.	**Audio** Listen to sections of the book read aloud.
Find out more about precipitation in your city.	Learn more about the history of the state.	Watch a video about the features of the state.	**Key Words** Study vocabulary, and complete a matching word activity.
Plan what attractions you would like to visit in the state.	Learn the full lyrics of the state song.		
Learn more about the early natural resources of the state.			**Slide Show** View images and captions, and prepare a presentation
Write a biography about a notable resident of North Carolina.			
Complete an educational census activity.			**Quizzes** Test your knowledge.

AV² was built to bridge the gap between print and digital. We encourage you to tell us what you like and what you want to see in the future.

Sign up to be an AV² Ambassador at www.av2books.com/ambassador.